Fun to Color

Louis Weber, C.E.O.
Publications International, Ltd.
7373 North Cicero Avenue
Lincolnwood, Illinois 60712
Ground Floor, 59 Gloucester Place
London W1U 8JJ

Permission is never granted for commercial purposes.

Customer Service: 1–800–595–8484 or customer_service@pilbooks.com

www.pilbooks.com

p i kids is a trademark of Publications International, Ltd., and is registered in the United States.

8 7 6 5 4 3 2 1

Manufactured in China.

ISBN-13: 978-1-60553-645-3
ISBN-10: 1-60553-645-8

Welcome!

This Fun to Color workbook has been specially designed to help prepare your child for school. You and your child should work together on each activity. In the front of the book, you will find simple, introductory exercises. As you work your way to the back of the book, the exercises will gradually become more complex and challenging.

Before you begin, show your child how to hold a crayon properly. Your child should pinch the crayon between the thumb and index finger. The side of

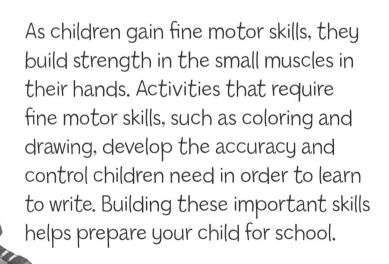

the crayon should rest against the side of the middle finger. As your child practices coloring this way, they will build important fine motor skills.

As children gain fine motor skills, they build strength in the small muscles in their hands. Activities that require fine motor skills, such as coloring and drawing, develop the accuracy and control children need in order to learn to write. Building these important skills helps prepare your child for school.

In addition to developing fine motor skills, the exercises in this book will challenge your child to identify colors, distinguish shapes, practice counting, and follow simple directions. To make the most of each activity, keep these suggestions in mind:

• Tear out the page along the perforation and lay it flat on your work surface. This will help your child focus on just one activity at a time.

• Read the directions aloud.

• Let your child attempt each activity and only assist when necessary.

• Be positive and encouraging. Learning should be fun!

When you reach the end of the workbook, celebrate your child's accomplishments. Remove the certificate of achievement and write your child's name on it so they can proudly display it.

Certificate of Achievement

I can COLOR!

Congratulations!

Taylor
(name)

has successfully completed the FUN TO COLOR workbook

Presented on _June 12_

Presented by _Mom_

Yellow

Color the white spaces YELLOW.

Draw a line around the YELLOW things.

Blue

Color the white spaces BLUE.

Draw a line around the BLUE things.

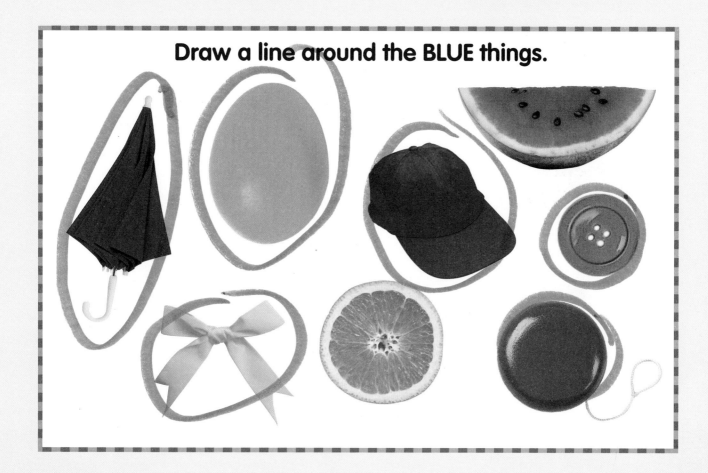

Green

Color the white spaces GREEN.

Draw a line around the GREEN things.

Red

Color the white spaces RED.

Draw a line around the RED things.

Orange

Color the white spaces ORANGE.

Draw a line around the ORANGE things.

Purple

Color the white spaces PURPLE.

Draw a line around the PURPLE things.

Brown

Color the white spaces BROWN.

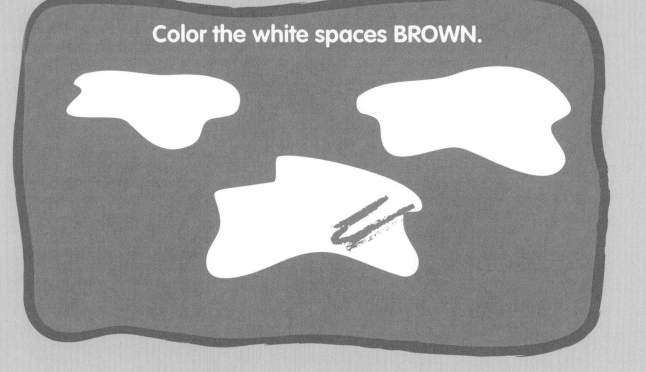

Draw a line around the BROWN things.

Black

Color the white spaces BLACK.

Draw a line around the BLACK things.

Square

Color the SQUARES blue.

Draw a line around the SQUARES.

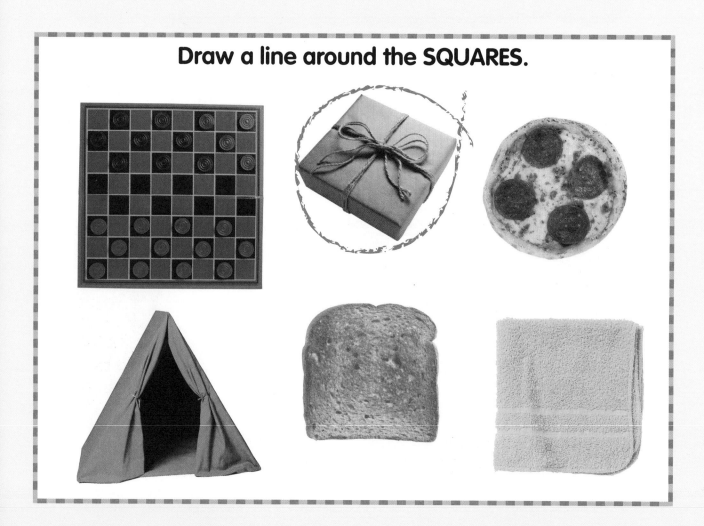

Circle

Color the CIRCLES red.

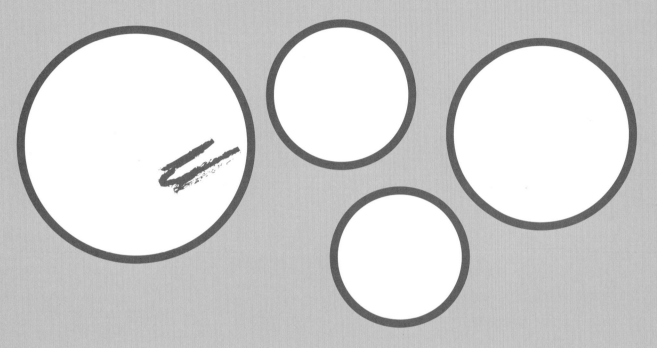

Draw a line around the CIRCLES.

Rectangle

Color the RECTANGLES orange.

Draw a line around the RECTANGLES.

Oval

Color the OVALS purple.

Draw a line around the OVALS.

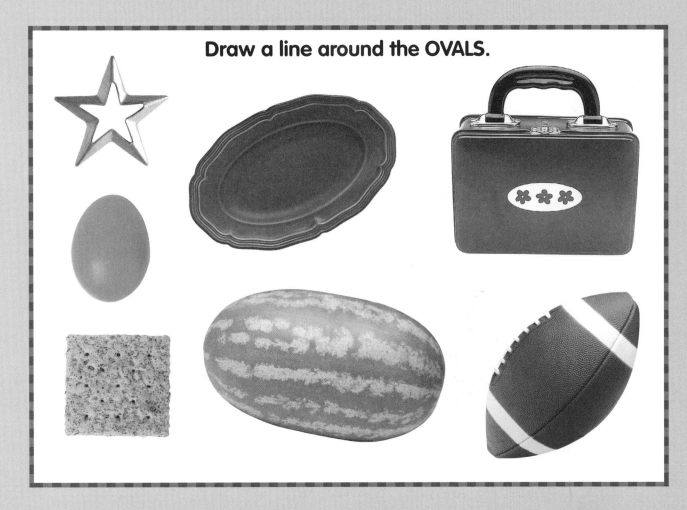

Triangle

Color the TRIANGLES green.

Draw a line around the TRIANGLES.

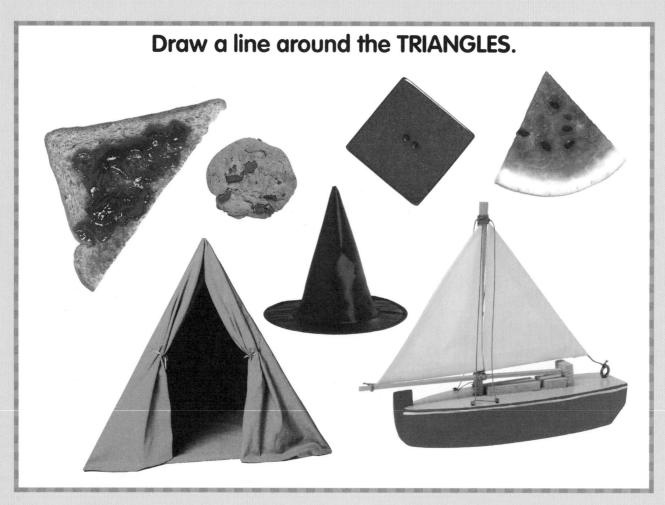

Heart

Color the HEARTS yellow.

Draw a line around the HEARTS.

Star

Color the STARS brown.

Draw a line around the STARS.

Diamond

Color the DIAMONDS pink.

Draw a line around the DIAMONDS.

Choose the correct color to complete the picture.

Choose the correct color to complete the picture.

Blast off!

Choose the correct color to complete the picture.

Whoo! Whoo!

Choose the correct color to complete the picture.

Choose the correct color to complete the picture.

Splish! Splash!

Choose the correct color to complete the picture.

Roooaaar!

Choose the correct color to complete the picture.

Choose the correct color to complete the picture.

What color is the whale?

What color is the crab?

What color is the frog?

What color is chocolate ice cream?

What color are palm leaves?

What color are the tiger's stripes?

What color is the school bus?

What color are the clouds?

What color is the shark?

What color are the giraffe's spots?

1 one

Count and color 1 truck.

1 one

Count and color 1 school bus.

2 two

Count and color the hot-air balloons.

2 two

Count and color the airplanes.

3 three

Count and color the sea horses.

3 three

Count and color the jellyfish.

4 four

Count and color the kites.

Count and color the clouds.

5 five

Count and color the sea stars.

5 five

Count and color the seashells.

6 six

Count and color the fish.

6 six

Count and color the spots on the turtle's shell.

7 seven

Count and color the leaves.

7 seven

Count and color the trees.

8 eight

Count and color the eggs.

8 eight

Count and color the butterflies.

9 nine

Count and color the birds.

Count and color the cattails.

10 ten

Count and color the flowers.

10 ten

Count and color the apples.

Use these colors to finish the picture:

Use these colors to finish the picture:

Use these colors to finish the picture:

Use these colors to finish the picture:

Use these colors to finish the picture:

Use these colors to finish the picture:

Use these colors to finish the picture:

Use these colors to finish the picture:

Use these colors to finish the picture:

Use these colors to finish the picture:

Certificate of Achievement

I can COLOR!

Congratulations!

_____
(name)

has successfully completed the FUN TO COLOR workbook

Presented on _____

Presented by _____

Certificate of Achievement

I learned a lot!

☐ I practiced coloring inside the lines.

☐ I matched colors.

☐ I identified shapes.

☐ I followed directions.

☐ I counted up to 10.

☐ I made my very own masterpieces!